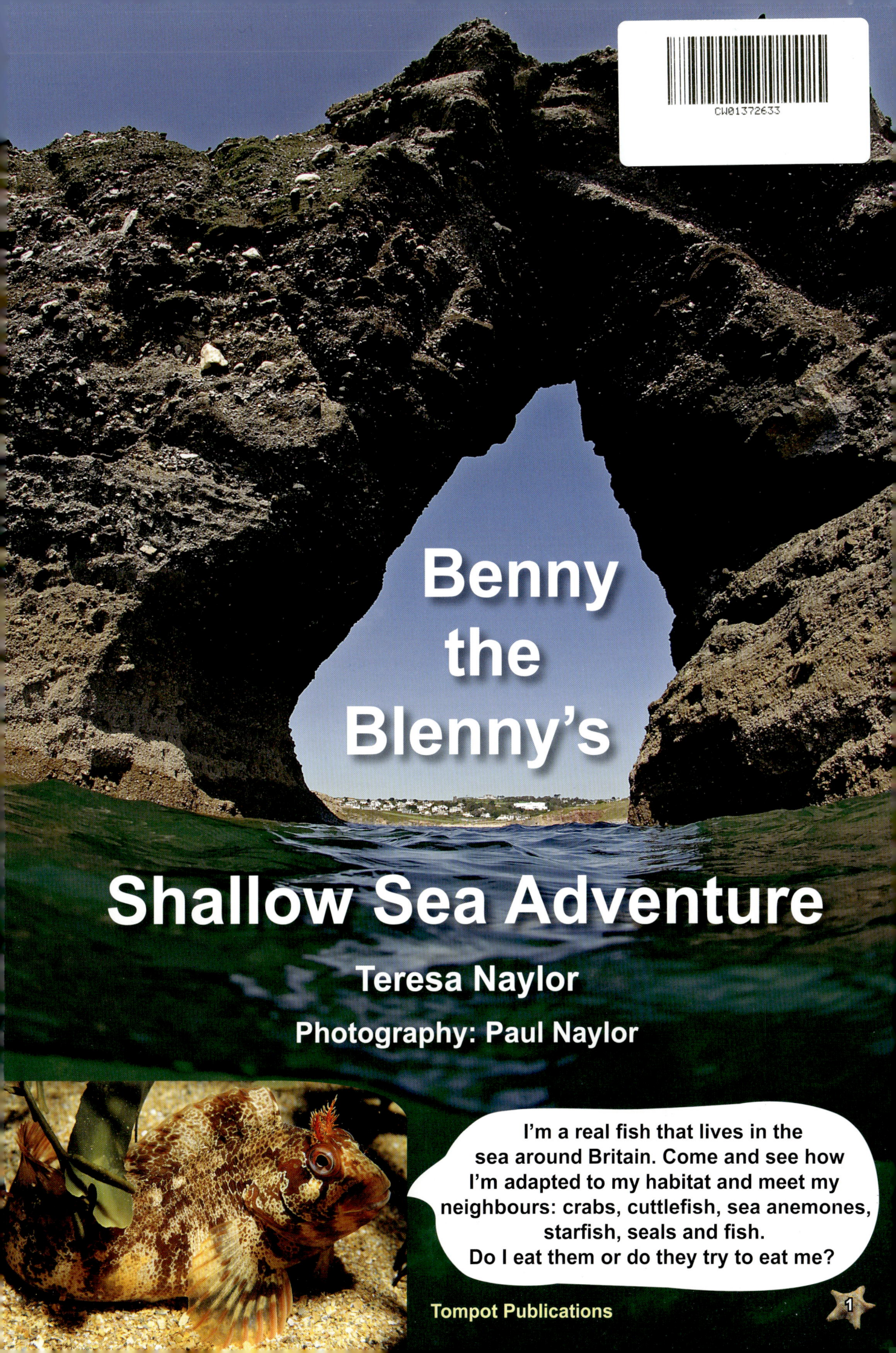

Benny the Blenny's Shallow Sea Adventure

Teresa Naylor

Photography: Paul Naylor

I'm a real fish that lives in the sea around Britain. Come and see how I'm adapted to my habitat and meet my neighbours: crabs, cuttlefish, sea anemones, starfish, seals and fish.
Do I eat them or do they try to eat me?

Tompot Publications

This book is dedicated to my beautiful granddaughter Felix. I am inspired by her enthusiasm for playing on the beach, exploring rock pools, learning about marine life and asking so many questions about 'Benny the tompot blenny'.

Acknowledgements
Thank you to Sam for his great patience and insight; and to Ellie, Ash, Emily and Dave for constructive criticism and answering late night 'how do I do this?' software queries. This book would not have come into being without Paul and his amazing photographs, my hero.

I am very grateful to Jack Sewell for using his tremendous skill to translate my thoughts into a stunning cartoon of 'Benny the blenny'.

Special thanks go to our wonderfully supportive friends who read painstakingly through the drafts and encouraged me in moments of concerned desperation: Cat, Di, Hazel, Hugh, Jane, Janet, Joe, Julie, Liz, Rachel, Sally and Sarah. Many thanks also go to numerous friends and their children on whom I foisted my plans for feedback.

Finally, I need to credit the tompot blennies who are such fascinating characters and started it all off!

First published in 2013

Copyright © 2013 cartoon and text Teresa Naylor
Copyright © 2013 photographs Paul Naylor

The right of Teresa Naylor to be identified as the author of this work has been asserted by her in accordance with the Copyright, Designs and Patents Act 1988.

All rights reserved. No part of this publication may be reproduced or used in any form or by any means - photographic, electronic or mechanical, including photocopying, recording, taping or information storage or retrieval systems - without permission of the publisher.

Published by
Tompot Publications
www.bennytheblenny.com

A CIP catalogue record for this book is available from the British Library

UK ISBN(print) 978-1-909648-00-5

Printed by Deltor in Cornwall UK

For enquiries and interest in e-books, whiteboard presentations and more about 'Benny the blenny' (including further food web information), visit www.bennytheblenny.com

For photographs and marine life information visit www.marinephoto.co.uk

Contents
Meet Benny 4
"My underwater world" 6
"The rock where I live" 8
"My home" 10
"The underwater photographer" 12
"Divers come to visit" 14
"That's close enough!" 16
"All about me" 18
"Who else lives on my rock?" 20
"My closest neighbours" 22
"Other animals living nearby" 24
"The slow edible crab" 26
"The view from my rock" 28
"What I like to eat" 30
"A large dangerous visitor" 32
"What eats me!" 34
"Thank you" 36
Glossary 38
Index 40
Find out more 41

When you go to the seaside, do you look out to sea and wonder what animals live beneath the waves? All is revealed in this book, it is a window into Benny the blenny's underwater world.

Meet Benny

Hello, I'm Benny the blenny. I'm a fish and I live in the sea near you. Come on an adventure to my underwater world. Find out more about me, where I live, what I like to eat, who my neighbours are and who likes to eat me!

Benny's actual size

About Benny

A blenny is a type of fish. Blennies like Benny have slimy skin with no **scales**, excellent eyesight and rows of small teeth like a comb. 'Combtooth blennies', which is the full name for his family, are found world-wide. Benny is a special type of blenny called a tompot blenny. Tompot blennies do not grow more than 30 cm long, and are usually much smaller, but they are real characters as you will see. You can tell tompot blennies apart from the other blennies that live in the sea around Britain by their colour, super-smart bushy head **tentacles** and the M-shaped spiky ridge between their eyes.

The name "tompot" is said to come from them being found in fishermen's crab pots (where they tried to eat the bait) and because they kept coming back like a **tomcat**! The scientific name for them is '*Parablennius gattorugine*' – what a mouthful!

Tompot blennies live on the bottom of the sea where there are holes or **crevices** they can hide in for protection. These hiding places are usually in natural rocky reefs or on stony seabeds, but they might be in shipwrecks or under **piers**. Tompot blennies are found around most of Britain, living in very shallow water next to beaches down to about 30 metres deep.

All the photographs in this book were taken in our beautiful British seas!

"My underwater world"

Welcome to my world under the sea. I live near the beach but it would be unusual to find me if you went looking in the rock pools. I live where the sea is just a bit deeper because I like my home to be covered by the sea all of the time!

Dog-whelk feeding on barnacles

Snakelocks anemone

Limpet

Thick top-shell

"The rock where I live"

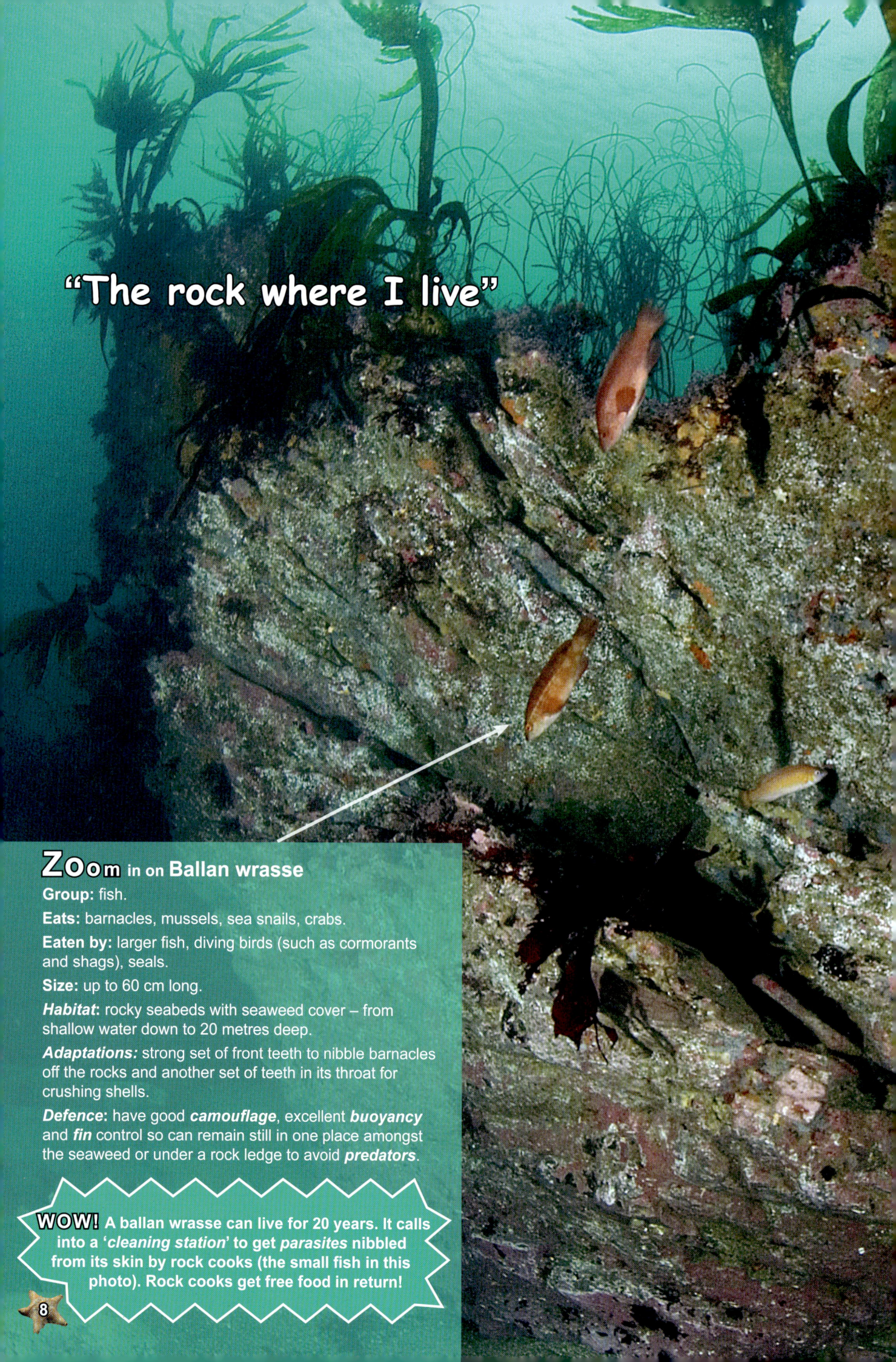

Zoom in on Ballan wrasse

Group: fish.

Eats: barnacles, mussels, sea snails, crabs.

Eaten by: larger fish, diving birds (such as cormorants and shags), seals.

Size: up to 60 cm long.

Habitat: rocky seabeds with seaweed cover – from shallow water down to 20 metres deep.

Adaptations: strong set of front teeth to nibble barnacles off the rocks and another set of teeth in its throat for crushing shells.

Defence: have good *camouflage*, excellent *buoyancy* and *fin* control so can remain still in one place amongst the seaweed or under a rock ledge to avoid *predators*.

WOW! A ballan wrasse can live for 20 years. It calls into a '*cleaning station*' to get *parasites* nibbled from its skin by rock cooks (the small fish in this photo). Rock cooks get free food in return!

This is where I live. My rock is taller than a person (2 metres) and the top of it is still covered by 2 metres of water at *low tide*. Have a good look around the rock, where do you think my home is? The larger fish swimming past are ballan wrasse, the small one is a rock cook.

"My home"

Look, I'm here! My home is in a crevice in the rock. When the sea gets rough or if a large fish comes along and tries to eat me, I wriggle to the back of my crevice and wedge myself in to keep safe.

> I spend a lot of my time watching everything from my crevice home. Can you see the barnacles feeding just in front of me? If I get very hungry I try to take a nibble at their feeding legs.

ZOom in on Barnacles

Group: *crustacean* - crab-like animals. Before 1830 it was thought that barnacles belonged to the sea snail group (*molluscs*).

Eats: *plankton* - *microscopic* plants (*phytoplankton*) and animals (*zooplankton*) that float in the sea.

Eaten by: crabs, dog-whelks, blennies, ballan wrasse.

Size: up to 3 cm across.

Habitat: rocks and large stones, shipwrecks and piers from the shore down to 100 metres deep.

Adaptations: cement themselves to the rock and make a 'house' out of their *armour plates*. There is a 'door' in the roof which they close to stop them drying up when the *tide* goes out.

Defence: if they sense danger (they can detect movement and changes in light levels) they will quickly close the 'door' to their armour-plated house.

WOW! Barnacles catch their food by waving their feathery legs out of the 'door' in the roof of their house. If you look at them close up, the legs look like a grabbing hand. The 'hand' is pulled back in very quickly if they are disturbed.

ZOom in on Humans

Group: mammal.

Eats: some eat crabs, lobsters, sea snails and fish, usually after cooking them. This human would rather just enjoy watching and photographing them.

Eaten by: nothing really.

Size: up to around 2 metres tall.

Habitat: widespread on land, go into shallow waters in the summer months to swim (some photograph marine life).

Adaptations: NONE (it's not their natural habitat!) so humans have to use equipment to survive under the sea – a mask (to see), fins (to move), *SCUBA* tank full of air (to breathe).

Defence: wet-suit to keep out the cold and to protect from scratches and stings.

WOW! Humans take a lot of things from the sea (fish to eat, oil for fuel, sand for building). Around Britain, we need to protect our marine life a lot better than we do now.

"The underwater photographer"

Zoom in on Moon jellyfish

Group: *cnidarian* – have *stinging cells*.

Eats: plankton.

Eaten by: squat lobsters, turtles – they sometimes mistake a discarded plastic carrier bag for a jellyfish. Unfortunately this can block the turtle's gut and kill them!

Size: up to 25 cm across.

Habitat: from the beach to open ocean.

Adaptations: their whole surface is sticky with *mucus* to help them catch plankton. They have 4 short central tentacles and many other tiny tentacles around the rim of their saucer-shaped body. Also around the rim, are *light sensors* to guide them towards or away from the sea's surface.

Defence: stinging cells – the sting is not powerful enough to bother humans.

WOW! Large swarms of many jellyfish are sometimes seen in the summer. This is because of the way they breed; stacks of miniature jellyfish develop on the seabed during part of their *life cycle* and they can all be released into the water at the same time when the conditions are just right. Swarms of jellyfish then get swept along by the sea's *currents*.

To be able to tell you my story, I needed underwater photographs. Paul is a diver and underwater photographer. Here, he is taking a photograph of a moon jellyfish. Can you see his camera? It is in a special case called a 'housing' which keeps the camera dry. The two long arms have *flashguns* on the ends of them which add more light to the photograph. It is darker underwater than it is on land. The deeper you go into the sea, the darker it gets.

"Divers come to visit"

Teresa is a diver too.
Here she comes now, swimming out from the shore to where I live. On the way to my rock she sees limpets, top-shells (sea snails) and two-spot gobies (small fish).

If she is lucky she might spot a cuttlefish on the way. She finds cuttlefish very interesting but they like to eat me, so I stay hidden in my crevice if they are around.

Teresa has found my rock but hasn't spotted me yet! She is using her torch to look at the barnacles feeding just below my crevice.

I've been watching her air bubbles and I've come out to see where they are all coming from. If Teresa puts her fingers too near me, I tap them with my nose to say: 'That's too close, keep your distance, it's my home!' Can you see the velvet swimming crab lurking further along the crevice? I have to watch out for him too!

"That's close enough!"

The divers come to look at what I'm doing but don't stay long because they cannot live under the water like I can. Paul takes the photographs and Teresa loves spending time watching me. They can only visit me when the sea is very calm. They must wonder how I cope when the sea is rough and there are huge waves crashing down and around my rock.

"All about me"

Dorsal fin
"This fin runs along my back. The **fin rays** (supports) are thick and strong with pointed ends, and can make the fin quite stiff. Along with my other fins, this helps me wedge myself into the back of my crevice if I feel threatened. I can use my fins to make me look bigger if a predator tries to eat me. This will also make me look more impressive to another blenny, whether I am in an argument or trying to attract a partner!"

Fin ray

Tail fin
"My tail fin helps me to swim fast when I need to. If I want to show off, I can fan the fin rays out to make my tail three times the size it is here."

Anal fin
"All of us use this fin for showing off to other blennies we want to impress. Males use special parts of their anal fin to look after the eggs they guard in their nests."

Pectoral fins
"These are rather like your arms. I use them to keep me in position, help move me along, lift my head up, display to other tompot blennies and wedge myself in my crevice. I'm a very good dad and also use these fins to fan clean water over the eggs that I guard."

Gill covers
"These protect my delicate gills, which take **oxygen** out of the seawater (like your lungs taking oxygen from the air you breathe in). The seawater comes in through my nostrils and mouth, passes over my gills and out under my gill covers back into the sea."

Head tentacles

"All of us tompot blennies, both males and females, have head tentacles. They are very sensitive and can detect chemicals in the seawater. The larger a male blenny's head tentacles are, the more attractive he is!"

Nostrils and nose tentacles

"I have two pairs of large nostrils between my eyes and the lower pair have a set of small tentacles just above them. You can also see many tiny nostril openings over the front of my head. All of these, along with my head tentacles, give me an excellent sense of smell to help me find food or a partner."

When the sea is rough, I stay hidden and safe from the pounding waves. My fins are strong and adapted to wedge me into my crevice home. I also find it easy to stay in position as I'm quite heavy. This is because, unlike fish that swim around all the time, I don't have a *swim bladder*. I only swim in short bursts but can do a bit of rock climbing by using my pelvic and pectoral fins to grip the rock.

Pelvic fins

"These are a bit like your legs. They are very strong and flexible (bendy) and I can use them for walking, wedging myself into my crevice or feeling for food down in the sand. If I want to get a better view of approaching predators or of something to eat, I use my pelvic fins to raise up my head."

"Who else lives on my rock?"

Connemara clingfish

Common lobster

Now the divers have gone, let's have a look at who else lives around my rock. It's a bit like a block of flats, each crevice has someone different living in it.

Spiny squat lobster

Leopard-spotted goby

Velvet swimming crab

20

Cushion star

Spiny starfish

Topknot

Young tompot blenny

Painted top-shell

Edible crab

"My closest neighbours"

Zoom in on Connemara clingfish

Group: fish.

Eats: small crabs, sea snails, shrimp-like animals and worms.

Eaten by: larger fish.

Size: up to 10 cm long.

Habitat: rocky areas, down to 30 metres deep.

Adaptations: has thick skin that can protect the fish if it is washed against the rocks. Body and head flattened so it can live in very narrow crevices. The pelvic fins underneath the front of its body are joined together to form a sucker.

Defence: keeps hidden away in its crevice and is well camouflaged.

WOW! The Connemara clingfish clings to the rock using its sucker (which works like a sucker on a bath toy) so it stays safe and does not get washed out of its home when the sea is rough.

I have some very close neighbours I'd like you to meet. A clingfish lives higher up the crevice where it is narrower. Two velvet swimming crabs live a little further down the crevice. If they come into my *territory*, I don't like it and I pester them until they go away.

Velvet swimming crab

ZOom in on Velvet swimming crab

Group: crustacean.

Eats: other crabs, sea snails, shrimp-like animals, small fish, worms and seaweed.

Eaten by: fish, cuttlefish, seals and humans.

Size: up to 10 cm across shell.

Habitat: among rocks and stones from the lower shore to 30 metres deep.

Adaptations: its back pair of legs are flattened like paddles and used for swimming. Fast moving so it can catch all sorts of *prey*.

Defence: always backs into its shelter with a sharp pair of claws at the front, ready to fight off any predator. If disturbed will attack rather than run away!

WOW! Velvet swimming crabs have bright red eyes and are sometimes called 'devil crabs'. They turn sea snails upside down and chip patiently away at the shell to get the flesh inside, just like you nibbling at an ice cream cone!

"Other animals living nearby"

You can see that the two velvet swimming crabs (the crabs with red eyes) are female because they are both carrying eggs between their body and tail flap. Just beyond them an edible crab has made its home. Below my crevice, nearer to the seabed, I often see a leopard-spotted goby who shares his hole with a spiny squat lobster. Can you see the squat lobster just behind the goby's head?

Eggs

Spiny squat lobster

25

ZOom in on Edible crab

Group: crustacean.

Eats: worms, clams and sea snails. It crushes shells with its powerful claws.

Eaten by: other crabs and lobsters when it has shed its shell to grow (*moulting*); otherwise by cuttlefish, conger eels, wolf-fish, other large fish, seals and humans! Very small ones are eaten by tompot blennies.

Size: these crabs can grow up to 25 cm across their shell (*carapace*) but rarely more than 15 cm.

Habitat: wide range from soft sand and mud, where they dig themselves in, to rocky reefs. From the shore to 90 metres deep.

Adaptations: flattened shell so it can back into crevices. Short but strong legs hook onto the rock to stay in position and help the crab to clamber up rock faces.

Defence: very thick shell. Backs into crevice and uses its heavy claws to form a barrier against any predator.

WOW! Edible crabs live for up to 20 years and large females can carry more than 2 million eggs at one time. Also known as 'pasty' or 'pie' crab because of the crimped edge around its shell.

"The slow edible crab"

Sometimes I see large edible crabs walking around the base of my rock.

This is me chasing off a small edible crab that has moved into my crevice. Can you see he is protecting his eyes and *antennae* with his large claws?

"The view from my rock"

This is what I can see from my crevice. In the early morning and late evening, I swim over here to go hunting for food. I move quickly across the seabed keeping hidden where I can. I like to eat snakelocks anemones but have to surprise them so that they do not capture me with their 'sticky' tentacles. The speckled fish is a ballan wrasse, he's big but I'm not scared of him as he prefers to eat sea snails and crabs.

Snakelocks anemones

Pink paint weeds

Leach's spider crab sheltering in a snakelocks anemone

Thongweed

Kelp

Zoom in on Snakelocks anemone

Group: cnidarian – have stinging cells.

Eats: small fish including gobies and young tompot blennies, prawns, crabs, anything that comes in reach of its 200 long snake-like tentacles. Each tentacle is covered with stinging cells that shoot out threads like miniature harpoons to catch prey.

Eaten by: tompot blennies, sea slugs and, when very young, by limpets and other sea snails.

Size: can grow up to 7 cm across the base and with its long tentacles outstretched can be up to 20 cm across.

Habitat: shallow rocky areas with plenty of sunlight, from the shore down to 20 metres deep.

Adaptations: microscopic plants (*algae*) live inside their tentacles and give the tentacles that green colour. The algae get protection and give the anemone some of the food they make using energy from sunlight (*photosynthesis*). This relationship is called *symbiosis*.

Defence: the stinging cells that help catch prey also sting any animal that tries to eat the anemone. Tompot blennies do not seem to be affected and will ferociously attack the anemone anyway!

WOW! In some parts of the world clownfish live in the sea anemones. Around our coast, we have a type of small spider crab that often lives among the tentacles of snakelocks anemones. The crab gets a safe home and a share of what the anemone catches; the anemone may gain some protection and food in return.

"What I like to eat"

Painted top-shell
3 cm across

Brittle-star
8 cm across

Isopod
0.8 cm

Long-clawed porcelain crab
0.5 cm across shell

Amphipod
0.6 cm

30

Hydroids
5 cm tall

Sea anemones
2 cm across

Here are some more animals and plants I like to eat. I find them using my eyes, my sense of smell and by feeling for them with my pelvic fins. I have very good front teeth for nibbling off bits of barnacles, anemone tentacles, worms and seaweed. At the back of my mouth I have other teeth for crushing the shells of small crabs, limpets and top-shells. I have a good varied diet and, as I eat both animals and plants, I am called an *omnivore*. When the sea is very rough, I have less choice of things to eat because I have to stay close to home.

Cuttlefish eggs
1 cm across

Paddleworm
20 cm long

Coralline seaweed
3 cm tall

31

"A large dangerous visitor"

If this seal caught me out in the open when I'm hunting, he would think of me as a tasty snack! So I have to keep my eyes open and, if there is a seal around, I stay well hidden in my crevice or under cover until he's gone.

Zoom in on Grey seal

Group: mammal.

Eats: fish, crabs and lobsters, sea snails, clams.

Eaten by: sharks, killer whales and humans (but only in some areas of the world).

Size: around 2 metres long, males tend to be larger than females.

Habitat: open sea, in the shallows and on beaches.

Adaptations: has two layers of dense waterproof fur and a layer of **blubber** (fat) under its skin to protect it from the cold. Very sensitive whiskers feel for food and sharp teeth help to catch it.

Defence: can swim very fast using powerful rear *flippers*.

WOW! The grey seal is able to hold its breath for about 12 minutes. Can be very curious about humans, often coming close to divers, small boats and walkers on the shore. Males are thought to live for 25 years, females for over 30 years. The oldest wild female on record was 46 years old.

"What eats me!"

Bass 60 cm long

Eek! Any of these animals would eat me so I have to be careful and hide at the back of my crevice when they come along. If I'm out hunting for my own dinner when they approach, I have to dash for home or find another place where I hope they don't spot me. My mottled colouring helps camouflage me. For predators that are only just a little bit bigger than me, such as a long-spined sea scorpion (another type of fish), I can make myself look too big to eat by sticking out my fins.

Pollack 50 cm long

Long-spined sea scorpion 20 cm long

Shag
75 cm long

Conger eel
150 cm long

Cuttlefish
25 cm long

Snakelocks anemone
20 cm across
including tentacles

35

"Thank you"

This is Benny's cartoon character who will appear in future books.

Where will his next adventure be?

Thank you for reading all about me. I think you will agree that I'm a very interesting fish. I have so much more to tell you. Please help me look after my home under the sea and the animals and plants that live with me. There are a few simple things you can do every day that will help. There are links to a list on my website www.bennytheblenny.com Maybe one day if you learn to *snorkel* (or SCUBA dive when you are an adult) you will be able to visit me in my home. I'm looking forward to that day.
Benny the tompot blenny.

GLOSSARY

adaptation - how animals or plants change slowly over time to become better suited to where they live.

algae - simple plants including seaweeds and those that grow as thin films on rocks in saltwater or freshwater.

antennae - thin stalks (sometimes called "feelers") found on the heads of some animals. Used to sense vibrations, smell, sound or heat.

armour plates - chalky hard sheet-like structures that are joined together to form a volcano-shaped house for a barnacle.

blubber - thick layer of fat under the skin of animals like seals, dolphins and whales.

buoyancy - the ability to float or rise in a liquid.

camouflage - the way in which an animal is coloured or patterned to blend in with its surroundings.

carapace - the part of a crab's armour that covers its back.

cleaning station - a place where fish go to have their parasites removed by 'cleaner fish'.

clownfish - a tropical fish, the famous ones have orange and white stripes and live in sea anemones.

cnidarian - type of animal with stinging cells. Sea anemones, corals, hydroids and jellyfish are cnidarians.

crevice - a narrow hiding place among rocks or stones.

crustacean - type of animal, without a backbone, that has a suit of armour (exoskeleton) and limbs with joints. Crabs, lobster, prawns, shrimps and barnacles are crustaceans.

current - the flow of water in a particular direction, often caused by the tides or wind.

defence - the way an animal or plant protects itself from being hurt or eaten.

fin rays - slender horny supports inside the fins of most fish.

fins - the structures used by fish for moving and steering.

flashguns - powerful lights that flash on for a fraction of a second to light up what is being photographed.

flippers - the webbed limbs of seals that they use for swimming.

food chain - the way plants and animals are linked together by feeding. Most food chains start with plants getting energy from the sun, this energy is then passed along the food chain.

food webs - a set of linked food chains that shows what eats what in a particular environment.

habitat - a specific area, small or large, that is home to a plant or animal and provides all its needs.

hydroid - type of animal with stinging cells, related to sea anemones, that forms tuft-like growths on seaweeds and rocks.

kelp - large brown seaweed.

life cycle - series of changes that an animal or plant goes through from first life to death.

light sensors - parts of an animal that detect if it is light or dark. Eyes are advanced light sensors.

low tide - the time when the sea reaches its lowest level, leaving the beach uncovered by the water.

microscopic - very small thing that cannot be easily seen with your eyes alone. A magnifying glass or microscope is usually needed.

mollusc - type of animal that does not have a backbone and has a soft body that is usually (but not always) protected by a hard shell. Limpets, whelks, winkles, sea slugs, mussels, oysters, scallops, cuttlefish, octopus and squid are all molluscs.

moulting - shedding of armour suit to allow growth, by crabs for example.

mucus - slimy fluid produced by animals to ease movement or trap food particles.

omnivore - animal that eats both plants and animals.

oxygen - the gas needed by almost all living things.

parasites - animal (or plant) that lives in or on another (the host) from which it gets food.

photosynthesis - process by which plants make food and oxygen from carbon dioxide and water, using energy from sunlight.

phytoplankton - microscopic floating plants that drift in the sea.

piers - large structures built out into the sea that serve as promenades, landing platforms or breakwaters.

plankton - plants and animals, mostly very small, that drift in the sea.

predator - an animal that hunts and kills other animals for food.

prey - an animal that is hunted and eaten by another animal.

scales - small overlapping plate-like structures that cover and protect the skin of most fish.

SCUBA - Self Contained Underwater Breathing Apparatus. Breathing equipment used by divers that doesn't need any connection to the surface.

snorkel - a J-shaped tube with a mouthpiece that lets you breathe while your face is underwater.

species - the smallest unit used when classifying animals and plants. A species can usually be thought of as a group of individuals that can breed among themselves.

stinging cells - specialised cells that fire out a tiny thread (like a harpoon) when triggered by movement or chemicals. They are used for both catching food and defence.

swim bladder - a gas-filled bag that helps a fish control its buoyancy.

symbiosis - close co-operation between individuals of different species, with both usually gaining from the relationship.

tentacles - slender, flexible, tube-like structures. In jellyfish and sea anemones, they are covered in stinging cells.

territory - an area which an animal treats as its own space and will defend against intruders.

tide - the rise and fall of the sea caused by the pull of the moon's gravity. The sun's gravity plays a smaller part.

tomcat - a male cat. They are known for returning to the same place to hunt time and time again.

zooplankton - animals, mainly very small, that drift in the sea. Some live there full-time, while others are the young stages of animals such as crabs, worms, sea snails, starfish, fish etc.

INDEX

adaptation	8, 11, 12, 13, 22, 23, 26, 29, 33
algae	29
amiphipod	30
armour plates	11
barnacles	7, 8, 11, 15
bass	34
blennies	5
blenny, tompot	every page!
brittle-star	30
camera	13
camouflage	8, 22, 34
carapace	26
clam	26, 33
classification	8, 11, 12, 13, 22, 23, 26, 29, 33
cleaning station	8
clingfish, Connemara	20, 22
cnidarian	13, 29
conger eel	26, 35
cormorant	8
crab	8, 11, 20, 21, 22, 23, 24, 25, 26, 27, 28, 29, 30, 33
crab, edible (pasty, pie)	21, 24, 25, 26, 27
crab, long-clawed porcelain	30
crab, spider	28, 29
crab, velvet swimming (devil)	15, 20, 23, 24, 25
crevice	5, 10, 15, 17, 18, 19, 20, 22, 24, 26, 28, 32, 34
crustacean	11, 23, 26
cushion star	20, 21, 24
cuttlefish	14, 23, 26, 34
defence	8, 11, 12, 13, 22, 23, 26, 29, 33
diving bird	8, 35
dog-whelk	7, 11
eggs, crab	24, 25
eggs, cuttlefish	31
eggs, tompot blenny	18
eyesight	5, 18, 31
fin ray	18
fins	8, 18, 19, 22
flashguns	12, 13
gills, gill covers	18
goby, leopard-spotted	20, 24
goby, two-spot	14, 29
habitat	8, 11, 12, 13, 22, 23, 26, 29, 33
humans	12, 14, 15, 16, 23, 26, 33
hydroid	31
isopod	30
jellyfish, lions mane	cover
jellyfish, moon	13
kelp	29
life cycle	13
limpets	7, 14, 29
lobster, common	12, 20, 26
mammal	12, 33
microscopic	11, 29
molluscs	11
mussels	8
nostrils	19
omnivore	31
oxygen	18
paddleworm	31
paint weed, pink	28
parasites	8
Parablennius gattorugine	5
photographer	12, 17
photosynthesis	29
phytoplankton	11, 13
plankton	11, 13
pollack	34
prawn	29
predators	8, 11, 12, 13, 22, 23, 26, 29, 33, 34
prey	8, 11, 12, 13, 22, 23, 26, 29, 30, 31, 33
rock cook	8, 9, 20
SCUBA	12, 37
sea anemone	7, 28, 29, 31, 35
seal	8, 23, 26, 32, 33
sea scorpion, long-spined	34
sea slug	29
sea snail	7, 8, 11, 12, 14, 21, 22, 23, 26, 29, 30, 33
seaweed, coralline	31
shag	8, 35
skin	5, 22
smell	19, 31
snakelocks anemone	7, 28, 29, 35
squat lobster, spiny	20, 24, 25
starfish, spiny	21
stinging cells	13, 29
sucker (clingfish)	22
swim bladder	19
teeth	5, 8, 31, 33
tentacles (blenny)	5, 19
tentacles (sea anemone, jellyfish)	13, 28, 29, 35
thongweed	28, 29
tide	9, 11
topknot	21
top-shell, painted	21, 30
top-shell, thick	7, 14
turtle	13
wolf-fish	26
worms	22, 23, 26, 31
wrasse, ballan	8, 9, 11, 20, 28
zooplankton	11, 13

40